Printed in China

ISBN 10: 0-618-90010-1
ISBN 13: 978-0-618-90010-7

3456789 1648 16 15 14 13 12 11 10

"Luis Garcia, meet Paula Lopez," said Mr. Delgado, the school librarian. "Having you two as my assistants is going to be great."

"Thanks," said Luis. He knew that Paula had been working as a student librarian for a week now, but it was his first day on the job. He felt slightly nervous.

"There's a lot to do," Mr. Delgado continued, "so you'll be 'partners in crime' around here."

Paula chuckled as she turned to Luis. "The only crime in this place," she said with a smile, "is putting the books away in the wrong order."

Mr. Delgado grinned, but Luis was worried. There were so many books to shelve! And they all had long, complicated numbers on them. How would he ever figure out how to do it right?

"Don't worry," said Paula. "I'm still learning how to do it, too. We can figure it out together."

"Let's hope so," said Luis.

"Like most school libraries," Mr. Delgado told Luis, "we use what's called the Dewey Decimal Classification system to organize and number our books. You'll find it makes a lot of sense. I'll see you two later."

"Let me show you the Dewey chart I'm making," Paula said to Luis. She pointed to a poster on the wall. It showed a circle with ten sections. The first section was labeled 000–099. The second one read 100–199, the third one read 200–299, and so on. But some of the sections were blank.

"The Dewey system organizes books by grouping them into ten main categories," Paula said. "Each category has a range of numbers. I still haven't filled in the numbers for some sections, though."

Read•Think•Write What numbers do you think the fourth through eighth pieces will show?

"The missing number groups are 300 through 399, 400 through 499, 500 through 599, 600 through 699, and 700 through 799," Paula said, as Luis wrote them in.

"We should add pictures," Paula suggested. "For example, books about art and sports are in the 700s, so we could add a picture of—"

"A soccer ball!" Luis said quickly, thinking of his favorite sport. "But shouldn't we start shelving first?"

"You're right," Paula agreed. "I always arrange them in numerical order on the carts."

"Sounds good," Luis said. "I'll start on this cart." He picked up the first book on the top shelf. It had the number 765 on its spine.

"That's the book's call number," Paula told him. "In the Dewey system, every book has to have at least three digits before the decimal point."

"These call numbers are really mixed up," Luis commented. "I have 765, 123, 516, 944, and 233."

Read•Think•Write Rearrange the numbers 765, 123, 516, 944, and 233 in numerical order.

"Got it!" said Luis after a little work. "In order from least to greatest they would go 123, 233, 516, 765, 944."

Just then, Mr. Delgado returned. "Could you compare these two lists of decimals and see if they match?"

"Sure," said Luis. "Paula, read your numbers out loud, and I'll compare them to what I have."

"Good idea," Paula agreed. "The first one is three hundred seventy-six and twelve hundredths."

Luis frowned. He was pretty sure that Paula meant the number 376.012, which was on his list, but something was wrong with the decimal.

Read•Think•Write What is the correct way of saying the number 376.012?

"Do you mean 'three hundred seventy-six and twelve thousandths?'" Luis asked Paula. "The third place to the right of the decimal point is always thousandths."

"Oh, right," Paula replied. "The first place to the right of the decimal point is the tenths, and the second place is the hundredths."

When they had finished comparing the lists, Luis asked, "So who's Dewey?"

"Melvil Dewey was an American librarian," Paula answered. "He invented his decimal numbering system in 1873. He was the first person to create a systematic way of classifying books. Mr. Delgado says this system is the most widely used one in the world."

"I'm sure it's a good system, but sometimes all the decimals get confusing," Luis admitted.

"I know," Paula agreed. "Hey, I've got five books here with really similar call numbers. Let's test each other. You pick out the one with the greatest number. Then I'll try to pick out the one with the least number."

"Okay!" Luis studied the books' numbers. They were 151.4, 155.154, 141.41, 155.54, 154.454.

Paula turned to Luis. "Okay, which number is greatest?"

Luis grinned. "Which is least?"

Read•Think•Write What is the order of the numbers from greatest to least?

“Out of all five, the least number is 141.41,” Paula decided.

“I agree. And the greatest number is 155.154,” said Luis.

Paula shook her head. “Look again, Luis. Remember, just because a number is longer doesn’t mean it’s greater.”

“I forgot that! The greatest number here must be 155.54, because fifty-four hundredths is greater than one hundred and fifty-four thousandths,” Luis corrected himself.

“That’s right,” Paula said.

Luis smiled. “I think I’m finally getting the hang of Dewey and his decimals!”

Responding Problem Solving

1. Understand Sequence Put the following whole numbers in order, from least to greatest: 641, 261, 164, 645, 426.
2. Write the number 708.57 in words, and write the number four hundred eleven and eight thousandths in digits.
3. Of the numbers 966.9, 966.009, and 966.99, which is greatest and which is least?
4. Which two of these numbers have a zero in the hundredths place? Which two have an eight in the thousandths place? 508.08, 187.008, 620.909, 300.068

Activity

Look at the numbers below. Write into a place-value chart only the numbers that have a four in the tenths place, the hundredths place, or the thousandths place:

035.849	410.4	645.293
166.47	537.834	724.043